Assurances

CRYSTAL BULLARD

ISBN 978-1-64114-945-7 (Paperback)
ISBN 978-1-64114-946-4 (Digital)

Christian Faith Publishing, Inc.
296 Chestnut Street
Meadville, PA 16335
www.christianfaithpublishing.com

Printed in the United States of America

Acknowledgements

Special thank you and love to my precious and always supportive mother, Dolores B. Bullard, my insightful advisor, Reverend James E. Satterfield and my brother and sisters.

Contents

When Will I Have Time?

I awake to go to work
Usually at the break of day
Meetings and delays, working for bills to pay
When will I have time?

I drive the freeways throughout the week
Going to school, work and play
Thinking of what I have to do all day
When will I have time?

I take care of the children
Do the cooking and cleaning
Washing, vacuuming, and sweeping
When will I have time?

I am going to school
Registration, bookstore, and four-hour class
Studying, homework, and attending labs
When will I have time?

I get together with colleagues, family, and friends
Party here and gather there
But the parties never end
When will I have time?

When will I have time?
After I've reached my destination?
At the end of a day of work
Once the children are asleep and chores are finished?
After you graduate from school
Once the parties are over and the money's been spent?

No, stop, look, and see
God's grace and mercy over thee
The place is here the time is now
Praise Him!

Today

What is on your agenda today?
Have you talked to Christ along the way?

Did you do what you want and not look back?
Or give thanks to Him for having your back?

Why is everything else so important?
And your Savior is only a remnant?

You are so busy doing this and that
Instead of praising God and that's a fact

You say you'll come to the Lord when you get straight
Yet day after day things get in the way

Don't you know who's watching over thee?
Why, why on earth can't you see?

There is nothing more valuable while on your way
Then communing with the Lord throughout the day

Is Your Life in Order?

Are you fighting for the right things?
Or is your life stuck in a sling

We fight for the wrong things
What difference does it make, what does it all mean?

Material things are not so important
No matter how powerful or potent

Come back home and stand still
Before you're out of control with your will

You know what you need to do
Get right and stop acting like a fool

Time is moving, it's drawing nigh
You'll want to commit while there's still time

The Lord is knocking at your heart's door
You ought to answer before life is over

Just Another Day

Is this just another day?
Where my time will idle away?

Do I talk with those who need me?
Or ignore they're humble plea?

Should I meet the needs of others?
Or question, why should I bother?

I say to myself, they'll find someone
I'm too busy so they get shunned

How is it that I could care less?
People need care, concern, and my best

Is this just another day?
Or will I show love to those who stray

Reflections

It's easy looking over there
Analyzing another
Reflections of oneself, "oh, brother"!

Inner turmoil and dissention within
A scattering mind around and again
Closed to change, I let nothing in

Less effort, agony and grief
Inward interactions leave them be
Outside distractions get no relief

Reflections of the past can bring hindsight
Whispers of confusion loud and clear
Seek perspective and insight

Reflections never lie
Change sweet change cannot be denied
Seek the Lord, He'll provide

Our Hurting Souls

Help us, Lord, oh, we pray
Help us to purge our hearts and minds today

To let go of our lust, alcohol, and drugs
We are yearning to get back to your unconditional love

We don't seem to know quite how to do it
We can't seem to realize you're waiting to prove it

We lean on our pride like it's a crutch
Instead it keeps us out of touch

We're in a tailspin wonder which way to turn
Knowing in our heart we have a yearn

Intervene, we pray, in our heart today
To take us off our hopeless pathway

Save us before we self-destruct
We totally realize we've run a muck

We plead to you, Lord, to please intercept
This evil within our wretchedness

Don't let us get caught out here in our sins
Save us and cleanse us, a new life to begin

Living Adjustment

Our lives are full of change
And they come with a varied range

We must adjust on our job
Even though we sometimes sob

We adjust to new places
And get familiar with new faces

As our lives change with age
We adjust to another phase

When will we adjust
To the one that's a must?

The one who is guiding
And always providing

The one who shines in our life
When we are blind and full of strife

Put your sights on the Lord
And read his holy word

He makes life worth living
Because he never stops giving

When we make the right adjustment
Then our life will be more content

Subtle Sickness

I am doing fine
That's what I tell myself
There's nothing wrong with me
On the outside, I know no one can see

I have a nice smile and a gracious tone
Clear eyes and a good demeanor
A straight stature and a smooth stride
How could you know I'm torn up inside?

The breakdown in communication with the one I love
Constant pressures at work and home
The defiance of children
Go over in my mind again and again

Feelings of loneliness and abandonment
I give my all over and over
Doesn't that count for anything?
Or is this just another problem I'm bringing

My nerves are on edge
My patience seems short
But I continue to work and deal with the greed
To fill the never ending needs

Sometimes I feel like I will explode
Or walk away from it all and just give up
I know I'm not the only one who feels this way
But I feel like I am, like a sheep gone astray

Will anyone truly hear this faint cry for help
Maybe not, so I leave my emotions to myself
Gnawing, eating me down to my soul
Lord, help me so that I can take hold

This subtle sickness that's deep down inside
I can't do it anymore, Lord, help me release my pride
Lord, you're the only one who can work with this sin
I'm receptive to your arms, please come on in

The Piece of a Man

Is your achievements all your own?
Stating that you've made it alone

You're told to make your way and set high standards
To chase after the dollar and not meander

At all cost you give up everything
To meet what you want no matter what it brings

Where are you going and what do you hope to find
Distance and busy work can be wasted time

Look close at who you are, what is really inside of you
And what is the driving force in what you say and do

See, your family's left without your love to share
You see their smiles but they are in despair

With all of your might and all of your power
You can't retrieve what you've lost in working hours

When are you going to look in your soul,
And see why you've put your heart on hold?

The piece of a man is like a puzzle of his life
If you place it wrong it will never fit right

Who puts the piece of a man back in place?
It's not you or I, it's not our place

If you are quiet and stand very still
You will hear the gentle voice of your inner man's will

Reminding you of your commitment of love and obligation
Come back in touch with God and your family without hesitation

It's that piece of a man that will never give in
The one called Christ who is there till the end

Are your achievements all your own, certainly not
It's the quiet one, the Lord, or have you forgot?

Empty Cup

No place to rest my weary head
From the far reaches of the earth to laying in my bed

Insatiable desires fill the thoughts of my mind
These driving forces make it hard to unwind

Back and forth time and again
Chasing insatiable when will it end?

Searching to quench these burning desires
Keeps me caught up in muck and mire

There's no answer out there, no, no such luck
Only a relationship with Christ fills the empty cup

There's Only One Way

There's only one way to cure a cold heart
It's not with people or material things
Or places that are far apart

There's only one way to heal the hurt and pain
It's not doctors or homemade remedies
Or pills you think will make you sane

There's only one way to erase resentment
It's not through a palm reader or horoscope
Or a psychiatrist that has good intent

There's only one way to love again
Its' not with a few drinks or drugs
Or sexual pleasures in the head

He says, "No one comes to the Father
Except through me," not Buddha, Allah
Or Hare Krishna you see

There's only one way to cure, heal,
Erase, and love again. Come as you are
Without one plea to the one who's waiting for thee

God promised to wash all your sins away
Through Jesus who died on the cross that day
To restore hope and draw you to Him to stay

Let the Past Be the Past

Let the past be the past, that is why it's the past
The past is not meant to last

The past is for reference, no place to dwell
Those negative thoughts feel like hell

It has been lived and now it is gone
Make the corrections from whatever went wrong

Stop dredging up old feelings that blind your sight
Let the past be the past, glean from the insight

Be glad for the past and the ability to go through it
It's meant to build character you know you can do it

The future is sabotaged when you keep looking behind
Enjoy the present, relish the time

Dwell on the joy and good times you had
Not on the things that made you sad or mad

The future is bright and ready to be explored
Close the door on the past and be receptive to much more

The Slaying Beast of Unforgiveness

Unforgiveness is a slaying beast
It engulfs your mind and drains your peace

It's a motivating drive that seeks to destroy
No matter what the cost and has a devastating ploy

This slaying beast is harsh and very cold
And it's story creeps and is subtly told

To somehow undermine and pay back
An unforeseen personal attack

While it eats at you and wears you down
Your facial expressions turn to frowns

You ache inside while it tears you apart
Limb from limb from the very start

It may hurt the other person, but mainly it hurts you
Because you won't let go of the unforgiving blues

It does not always affect the other person
But it will cause our health to somehow worsen

An unforgiving person, it wasn't meant to be
Endless persecution will take it's toll as you can see

The beast of unforgiveness when it is truly done
Will have destroyed the loving heart of the unforgiving one

Forgive, Why?

Oh, help me, Lord, to forgive
To not hang onto tales and fibs

Mistrust and conflict lead to anger
Turmoil and adversity makes loved ones strangers

Why relive the hurt over again?
When it first happened, you didn't like it then

Why wear this arrogance like it is a badge
Rubbing it in others face so it can last

The pain festers in your heart and mind
When you won't let go and remain unkind

Holding on to such an awful feeling
Has no purpose or lasting meaning

When does a person ever realize and see
Non-forgiveness continues to hurt you and me

It robs you from really enjoying today
And puts your future on delay

Yes, forgiveness will erase another's transgressions
But it's more for you to grow in the lesson

Forgiveness is not just for the other's relief
But a reminder that Jesus continues to forgive thee

Take a Bit Out of Bitterness

Start the healing process within
Forgive the one who hurt you
Forgive the one who misunderstood you

You cannot change the past it is gone
Don't leave it alive through hurts
Let it go and start a new

Live above the words and accusations
You are being eaten alive by the acid of bitterness
It is vengefully exhausting and painful

Bitterness is consuming you
Your bitterness is changing you
It has changed who you are

Bitterness has changed your life
You can have peace and joy again
Lord, grant me the strength to forgive the hurts

I want to go on with my life
Help me to release this rearview mirror
Clear away this trash that lays waste in my mind

You sacrificed all to forgive me
And continue to forgive me daily
Help me, Lord, to walk in the spirit of forgiveness

A Grain of Sand

Oh, how I wonder how it could be
That God would notice a grain of sand like me

I sit in awe and in dismay
That he chose me one special day

What is it, what do I really have
That makes him feel so glad?

It's that I accepted Jesus, God's gift of love
His love of salvation that was sent from above

My heart sings for his marvelous grace
Because he was willing to take my place

Thank you, thank you for all you do
And for what I am, now with you

A little speck, like a grain of sand
Is somebody special in God's loving hand

Quiet Spirit

I long for the quiet spirit in me
These days shake me with fallacies
Temper this longing heart of mine
So that my inner eyes can see

Uncertainties rack my wondering mind
What is ahead on this path of life?
Solid ground is where I seek to reside
In tune with the pulse of time

Come and settle my roaming soul
I know I will begin to grab hold
Fall fresh deep down within
Let my quiet spirit soar again

In the Fog

Now and then I feel like I'm in a fog
Almost as if I've been drinking grog

So unsure and so out of touch
Even thinking my life isn't much

It seems like such a winding trail
That I wonder if I will ever prevail

People around me get in my face
And the way we are moving at such a fast pace

Like a merry-go-round going round and round
How my heart longs for solid ground

I can't see the forest for the trees
I know it's time to get on my knees

I look to the hills because I've been told
That Jesus's promises will break strongholds

He comes to the rescue to fight every war
For the sick, the lonely, and the poor

He reaches to touch the downtrodden
To let me know I'm not forgotten

As the fog begins to lift from my eyes
I rejoice in knowing he's drawing nigh

My heart begins to sing and shout
Hallelujah to the Lord, there's no doubt

The Thirst of the Soul

There is a thirst hidden within
That you often try to quench

An unusual persistent thirst that you
Constantly try to drench

A thirst that isn't simply satisfied
By things you try by day or by night

It's drenched with clothes, money, boats, and cars
Jewelry, jobs, or travel through the stars

What about food, sex, liquor, drugs, and such
Searching and seeking to fill the quenchless cup

Once you think it's been found
You think you've gotten off the merry-go-round

Only to find you're back in your ride
Seeking to quench the thirst inside

No matter what road you venture on
Satisfaction is temporary and so you move on

The thirst comes from the one within
With you a relationship he longs to begin

You were created with an emptiness inside
That can only be filled by your union with Christ

Only Jesus can fill your thirsty soul
Quenching the yearnings with mercies untold

Don't Give Up on Love

Don't give up on love
We need your love to uplift us
And to give us strength

Don't give up on love
Sometimes it's hard to give
But we need yours to carry on

Don't give up on love
Don't take away your love
It helps us through a day

Don't give up on love
We are depending on yours
Even when it hurts

Don't give up on love
It's a life raft when others fail
Just knowing your love is there

Don't give up on love
It's wonderful and nurturing
And yours is needed most

Please, don't give up on us
I won't

The Best Piece of the Pie

In life there are many facets
Many pieces of the pie
Different roads of life to tread
I don't always know why

Each aspect is important
Every piece has its place
From work, education, and status
To finding a living space

I have thought about every act
And calculated every move
There is precision in my actions
To insure everything goes smooth

Working hard to build
This little empire of mine
Where all of my needs are met
And all the pieces are aligned

In this empire I have built
There is a crack in my foundation
A piece of the pie is missing
I have missed my declaration

I haven't accepted Jesus Christ
As the cornerstone of my soul
To solidify the best piece of the pie
To make the pieces whole

Will Anyone Cry

If you were all alone today
And knew no one at all

What would you think of first?
Where'd you go when you fall?

What do your words express?
Are they negative and harsh?

Is it all about you?
Are you the only important part?

Who needs people, what does it really matter?
People are our life, without them life is sadder

The cultivation of relationships are who we really are
Without the love of others, we are like an empty jar

Will anyone cry when your life is said and done?
The love you shared throughout life, your loved ones

Lost and Found

Where do I go when I have no place to turn?
How do I release the bad things that I've learned?

Who do I talk to about where I went wrong?
And how ashamed I am all day long

Is there someone out there
That I can talk with and share

I share with my friends of my pain and sorrows
And how unsure I am of tomorrow

Tell me tell me what do I do
When everyone you talk to is the same as you

Jesus is calling saying come to me
And I will set your poor soul free

Free from the torment and the fire
And grant me my heart's desire

This is a promise he freely expresses
Worship and praising him releases my stresses

I've accepted Jesus and am no longer running around
I was lost and confused but now I'm found

Can We Ever Make It Right?

As we travel through our life, we have a series of choices
Based on the consequences, we realize some aren't the best voices

These choices could affect a family member or friend
The words are said in the heat of a moment a bad message is sent

There are many broke down relation-
ships, due to unresolved hurt and pain
Can we possibly make amends and truly begin again?

From whatever time or unclear reason
After hurting each other we give up our allegiance

Please try in your heart to release the words that bind
Let us start anew so that we can love each other again

Jesus died and forgave, an example of what to do
If we're honest with ourselves, we can forgive too

Can we build the bridge to our love again?
Or does the closeness really have to end

There is hope on the horizon, I see it coming through
A genuine relationship, building once again with you

Why Don't I Love Myself?

Is it when I was young
The other children made fun

Or when I was a teenager
And being put down was always major

Not being pick for the team
Felt awful and downright mean

Self expressed put downs of mine
That were never really fine

Or longing to talk to Dad about plenty
But he wasn't around, which made me empty

Or the friend who promised not to tell
And told your special secrets, that was hell

Was it when you looked at yourself in the mirror
And thought you looked even bigger

No wonder I am so confused
Living on others abuse

That is why I am out of whack
Listening to others value stack

What does it matter what others think?
When most of the time their opinion stinks

I am one of a kind and a special part
Of creation right from the very start

I wasn't an error or a mistake
I was meant to be here from the gate

There is no other person quite like me
I've got Christ approval you see

He loves me and He lets me know
So those negative opinions have to go

Why don't I love myself, is there a reason?
No, God's love erases all reasons

A Void for Jesus

There is a void, I'm unsure why
That can't seem to be filled
I've played and I've had fun
But yet I question my will

No matter what I do to quench
There's still this emptiness
I seem happy on the outside
But inside there is still unrest

What can I do?
To fill this void inside
Can anyone else feel it?
My heart begins to sigh

My desires are not for what I see
They're not for what I want
I lust for things all the time
But in the end, they only taunt

God's love is what is missing
Jesus's love is the void
He left it just for him
And it's not to be destroyed

So no matter what you do
Or what void you try to fill
Nothing else can replace
Jesus's love, and that's for real

Jesus's Way

Jesus shows me how to love
How to love my mate
How to love my children
How to love my friends
How to love others
How to love myself
How to love Him
How to anticipate and love eternal life
Jesus is the way, the truth, and the life
Thank you, Lord
Praise your holy name

What Will Last

Send a thinking-of-you note out of the blue
To let someone know, I'm thinking of you

Telling your loved ones of the love in your heart
To give them assurance whether near or apart

Giving your children a hug and a kiss
So often that they won't have to miss

Rebuilding a broken relationship
While out on a short weekend trip

Being a hero by saving the day
By assisting someone along the way

Giving encouragement, support, and hope
To someone who's on their last rope

A gentle touch and a warm embrace
That will put a smile on a face

The sincere prayers from others who care
Spreads comfort and joy anywhere

The covenants of Jesus, whose promises are true
They're tailor-made for me and for you

Christ will exalt you if you trust in his name
Your faith will mean more than power or fame

Great are these gestures when they are put forth
It makes life a major part of our worth

Give generously and give in mass
Only what you do for Christ, is what will last

The Fire Within the Flame

You started out charged up and ready to go,
Who had the right answers, who was to know

From the very beginning there were hills to climb,
You were determined to climb, time after time

You hung in there and you left your mark
Without you knowing it, you've touched their heart

There were times when you'd thought to throw in the towel
Even though you were blindsided, you'd make it somehow

The journey's been long and often rough
And it's built your character, but made you tough

You often wonder how you made it out there
You're family was at home on their knees in prayer

Prayers for protection, guidance, and a shield
To give you strength, so they wouldn't break your will

There is a Savior so strong and so true
He will protect and lead you through

He's not out there, way out somewhere
He's in your heart and he's waiting to share

Your inner most cares and all your concerns
With him you can relax, and yet you will learn

No one makes it on might and power alone
But by the Spirit, for he shields his own

As you can see, you can't begin to please man
But you can with the Lord, once you decide to begin

This anticipated journey, no one else can walk
The one meant for your heart-to-heart talk

You've given up on Christ though he hasn't on you
He's still waiting for that connection with you

Yes, you have arrived, but I think you should know
It's been Jesus Christ, only Christ that has made you glow

It Was Never Me

It was never me
It was always thee
Taking care of me
And forgiving me

It was never me
It was always thee
How happy I can be
Knowing it is thee

It was never me
It was always thee
Watching over me
So carefully

It was never me
It was always thee
I give praise to thee
For your love endlessly

You've protected me
Always guiding me
With angels encamped that's thee
Guardians just for me

A special love I see
Given by only thee
Grateful as I can be
Now and eternally

Oh Lord
Thank thee
Thank thee

Country Love

An unexplainable love of compassion
A deep love for your fellow man
Taking responsibility and action
As only a service man can

Giving freely and giving it all
Not with selfish concern or gain
Fighting the battle willing to fall
Serving and protecting America's name

You walk tall you walk with grace
Though struggles may be nigh
You see the pride all over your face
As you give it one more try

Thank you thank you service man
So loyal and so true
For expressing your country love
In all you say and do

Anyone Can

When you look around the neighborhood
What is it that you can see?
Someone lending a helping hand
Reaching out to others, doing whatever he can

Once he was rough, and hard to get along
Mean and spiteful, and did what was wrong
Drinking, drugging, a spirit of mistrust
Throwing his weight around and didn't take no stuff

Quiet and to himself, with a strong and sturdy look
After a few moments, he can read you like a book
The streets have taught the lesson and he learned them very well
You couldn't do him wrong or you'd be faced with hell

Seems like such a long time ago, the way he used to be
No one really knows him, unless he let's you see
Sometimes when he's ready, he'll invite you to come in
And as he gets comfortable with you, he shows that great big grin

His exterior is tough, but he has a giving heart
Reaching out to his community from dawn to dark
Encouraging drug addicts and filling in the gap
Directing children on there way to school, to choose the right path

Don't think you're invisible or that you can't be seen
The loving things you do, while you're acting cold or mean
You want nothing but the best, for those that pass you by
Sometimes things hurt you to your heart, and all you do is sigh

You have established your place, in the area that you reside
And when you start to witness, you do it with pride
To anyone, this comes to you to say
You're appreciated and respected in a very special way

You've been touched and transformed
In a wonderful way by God
On the battlefield for the Lord
You've gracefully accepted your job

Mama

As I think of her fondly going through my mind,
I laugh at the latest enjoyable time

I think of laughing, hugging, kissing,
That it's beautiful like a warm wind whistling

My feelings for her are a fond affection,
When I ponder with deep reflection

I wonder how love can be so deep,
And knowing it's something I simply must keep

It keeps me going day in and day out,
And gives me comfort without a doubt

Freely sharing and freely giving,
A zest for life and for living

As I look in her eyes, I see such compassion,
That reveals her heart of love and passion

How can I express how I feel,
To a love that is so very real

Simply, words seem not enough,
And getting them out right, seems somewhat tough

Mama, Mama, how do I say,
That you're my life in so many ways

What is in my heart is what's in my soul,
To give, to cherish, and to hold

I relish in our love so fine,
That engulfs my mind time after time

Her love is mine and it's not at a loss,
And I will hold on to it at all cost

From the bottom of my grateful heart,
Thank you for your love from the start

Mama, I just want to say without choking up,
Your love has been some powerful stuff

Thank You, Mom

Thank you, Mom, for being there each and every time,
No matter what, when, or where, your being
there gives me peace of mind

Thank you for the joy you've shown in all that I have done,
Whether attempting a sport or creating a
work of art, we enjoyed it all in fun

Thank you for loving me deeply, honestly, and true,
For being gently supportive in all you say and do

Thank you for encouraging me when I felt so frail and weak,
Lifting me up and brushing me off, when you did not speak

Thank you for showing me the pride of a loving family,
Even with our ups and downs, you pro-
moted hugging instead of frowns

Thank you for saying good-bye, when it was so hard to do
Keeping open arms of love, until I came back to you

Thank you for not giving up on me when
my decisions were in doubt
You kept on working with me, until I could see my way out

Thank you for showing me how to respect
and treat others in any situation
Even with those that are hard to love, you have been
my inspiration

Thank you for teaching me a consistent spiritual foundation
Seeing you praying on your knees was my
life raft through life's degradation

Thank you for singing songs of praise to the Lord on high
Lifting him up so thankfully, made me feel warm inside

Thank you for the simple life, that instilled
life's lessons and pleasures,
Cultivating, molding, and making an adult
that could storm any weather

Thank you for having my back with lots of moral support
It has meant so much from day to day,
when I'm out here trying to sort

Thank you for saying, "I love you," again and again and again,
To reassure me that your love will never come to an end

Thank you, Mom, for being you, this priceless love of mine
Plenty loving, sharing, kissing, caring, I am
grateful you are mine all mine

Peace in Pain

There once was fun, laughter, and lots of cheers,
Now Mama is no longer here

She passed just before the winter holidays
Now my mind is filled with haze

Life was so wrapped up around her
Since then things seem like a blur

Who would know there would be such emptiness?
And feeling my heart is in such distress

The pain is so deep and so hard to bear
My days are full of pounding despair

I miss you, Mama, I miss you so,
Unsure what to do, cause I feel so low

My mind meanders and I am so lost
I couldn't have imagined there'd be such a cost

Oh Lord, transition this ache inside,
So this pain will gradually begin to subside

Lord, I can't help but thank you for the marvelous gift you gave
That precious gift of a mom, who's been called home to stay

Reverend, the Professor of the Soul

He preaches of the sacrifice the Lord made for us all
Giving insight to the mind to break down satanic walls

He talks about strongholds, and that they are for real
If you don't get prepared, your soul he will steal

He teaches of the magnitude in the pages of the Word
Question after question, he answers from simple to absurd

His instruction is precise and he never deviates
From Christian to Atheist, he sets the record straight

The Word of God is refreshing to a receptive heart
Those who seek to understand what their life is all about

A wellspring of understanding begins to open wide
With the Holy Spirit's guidance, we start to change inside

His lesson states the walk is hard, but we must endure
Our reward is the Crown of Life, that you can be sure

Do not stray and don't give up, you're on the right road now
The Lord loves you and he gives you strength to make it some how

His covenants and his promises will stand the test of time
Those that won't accept his Son, their punishments a crime

Yet none have given the ultimate, though that was his call
The Son of God, Jesus Christ, the greatest one of all

Endless mercy, grace, and love is hard to understand
No one on earth can give the pure love that God can

Thank you, Lord, for the reverend and the Word he's taken hold
The Word he preached has helped to cleanse our sin sick soul

Rejoicing in the Holy Spirit

The joy of rejoicing is such a lovely state of mind
It's comforting and renewing and one of a kind

No matter where I am or when I'm in doubt
This rejoicing state of mind gives me mental clout

I marvel in the union the Holy Spirit provides
Uplifting, transforming, he's always by my side

I'm caught up in the splendor, there's pep in my stride
That is personally granted by my Savior Jesus Christ

Lingering Moments
with the Master

I freely let go of cares and worries
And will not be in any kind of hurry

I rest my head on your breast
It is where I find the sweetest rest

Abide in me as I feel your presences
Sustain me with your precious essence

I relish in these lingering moments
Engulfed in the Lord's loving solace

Comfort in Daily Blessings

The provisions of the Lord cannot be denied
There's comfort in know he's by your side

Like lying in your favorite bed
And the joy you feel when you rest your head

Like watching water tranquil and blue
Or having your favorite food to chew

Like reading the words of a love letter
Touching your heart like no other

Like the smile of a child as they take their first step
Realizing with the Lord, you know you've been kept

Like reaching out to help one another
Always makes you feel much better

But the ultimate comfort of love blows your mind
It's the love of the Lord to the end of time

A Steadfast love

A steadfast love
So rich and sincere
A precious love
That I hold so near

A steadfast love
That is one of a kind
It is so intricate and so divine

A steadfast love
So deep yet new
It keeps me running back to you

This steadfast love
What a revelation
I cling to its strong foundation

A steadfast love
A covenant of peace
Will always keep my heart at ease

The Lord made a covenant and it can't be removed
His steadfast love is for me and you

Look What the Lord Has Done

Look what the Lord has done
He's changed this cold empty heart of mine
And changed others too time after time

Look what the Lord has done
No matter who comes through the door
He always has room for one more

Look what the Lord has done
He points us toward his mighty cross
For all to view that are lost

Look what the Lord has done
He sheds his light where there is none
Calling on those whom are willing to come

Look what the Lord has done
He spreads his love, mercy, and grace
To all whom are burden and displaced

Look what the Lord has done
He draws us to his marvelous light
And fills us with wisdom and insight

Look what the Lord has done
A sturdy relationship he steadily builds
Gently transforming our inner will

Look what the Lord has done
Now we are one, what a glorious undertaking
His plans for us are always in the making

While I Still Have My Breath

While I still have my breath
I will lift up holy hands

While I still have my breath
I will share all that I can

While I still have my breath
I will give unselfishly

While I still have my breath
I will show myself worthy

While I still have my breath
I will pray throughout the day

While I still have my breath
 I will follow the light of his way

While I still have my breath
I will tell those that I meet

While I still have my breath
About the one that is so great

While I still have my breath
I will follow his light and love

While I still have my breath
I will worship my heavenly love

While I still have my breath
I will strive to be on one accord

While I still have my breath
I will praise and thank the Lord

While I still have my breath
I will love and cherish the one
Jesus Christ, God's only begotten Son

You're a Gem in God's Eyes

When you think no one loves you, just remember
You're a Gem in God's eyes

When you think nobody cares, just remember
You're a Gem in God's eyes

When you are lonely with no one to love, just remember
You're a Gem in God's eyes

When you think you're ugly and unattractive, just remember
You're a Gem in God's eyes

When you're in pain and all is gone, just remember
You're a Gem in God's eyes

When you think you're a failure, just remember
You're a Gem in God's eyes

When you think you've done very wrong, just remember
You're a Gem in God's eyes

When you've been abused and lost hope, just remember
You're a Gem in God's eyes

When you have no place to turn, just remember
You're a Gem in God's eyes

When you want to give up on life, just remember
You're a Gem in God's eyes

He loves you no matter who you are, what you've done, when you
did it, where you've been, or why you are there, just remember
He gave his all, his only begotten Son because of his love for you

So when you're at your lowest point, look up and call of him first
Allow him into your heart and experience his sacred love because
You are a Gem in the eyes of God

Lord, Thank You for My Trials

The impact of pain is a familiar sight
It comes in many ways and causes much strife

All around me is hatred and anger
It is seen, heard and often has danger

The trials of life are sometimes hard to bear
These pains produce a lot of wear and tear

There's no way out, no means of escape
From the painful lessons I must partake

Why are problems and conflict such a way of life?
Envy, suffering, toil, and strife

Troubles, failures, misery, and hurts
I often wonder, *What's it all worth?*

There is no announcement when troubles come
I'm just blindsided and left feeling numb

The lessons of pain I've learned to see
Because they are tailor made for me

The things that hurt also instruct
And let me know I don't live off of luck

How frail I am and my days are few
So it's important to learn and be renewed

I will not try to dodge or escape
What is meant to teach and set me straight

I am learning little lessons every day
To help me adjust to trials along the way

There's love, guidance, and grace in these lonesome steps
And I see God's hand correcting the mess

Thankful and grateful for these lessons of mine
That are humbling and molding me in to one of his kind

A kind of person that is pleasing to God
When the lesson is learned, he approves with a nod

No Words

There are no words in the heart of a man
To express the love that the Lord has designed

You can search your mind for the right words to say
But they're not adequate nor do they convey

Such a magnificent, majestic, enormous love
That I get lost in it from just one little hug

It takes my mind and my breath away
That I relish in one touch all day

My heart sings a song of joyous praise
That sometimes makes me stop and gaze

I'm in awe and yet I can't quite explain
How I love the Lord Jesus and his holy name

There are no words, no not one
To truly express what God has done

God's Garden

A garden full of life's beautiful essence
That blossoms from life's lessons

Precious fruits of peace, joy and temperance,
Meekness, goodness, faith and gentleness

Planted are the pearl seeds from grace
In our cultivated souls over time and space

Righteousness and praise spring forth from the garden
Love and longsuffering are some of its harvest

Embrace your garden so divinely sown
Cherish the blossoms that our Lord has grown

Not Alone

There is a struggle in my mind
That I fight with all the time

This conscious struggle is right from wrong
I fight with it all day long

The struggling I have is with sin
Fighting, pushing, who will win?

I am constantly struggling with my flesh
Who is always trying to say yes

My spiritual man tells me I have sense
Don't cross over that costly fence

The struggle of this force is so strong
I question if I can come out unharmed

There is one thing that is known
I don't have to fight this struggle alone

I have a righteous advocate
Whom sometimes I often forget

He guides me down the right path
To shield me from a satanic attack

He is always available when I call
And picks me up when I fall

He's the third person of the Trinity
The Holy Spirit takes good care of me

The Solace of Prayer

As I close my eyes to pray and unwind
I draw in my wandering mind

Stop all idle thinking and become very still
To listen to the Lord's marvelous will

When I think of whom I'm going to address
It causes my fleeting spirit to rest

I lift up the Lords name in thanksgiving and praise
Grateful for the vessel of prayer and amazed

My being and soul are rejuvenated
Fears melt away like I anticipated

This union is so wonderful and amazing to see
The uniting of the Holy Spirit and a wretch like me

Words seem inadequate to express this union
It's as precious as when taking communion

Prayer, precious prayer transforms the old to the new
It keeps me constantly in love and touch with you

A Living Vessel

Use me Lord this I pray
To strengthen another along the way

Help me Lord as I strive to be
A servant who pleases thee

Grant me the wisdom to clearly hear
Your guiding words that keep me near

Lead my steps to your marvelous light
To assist others who have lost their sight

Fill me Lord with your loving grace
To share with others who have been displaced

Open my heart to your purpose so grand
A strong foundation upon which to stand

I'm standing firm with a gentle spirit
Sharing your love with all who will hear it

Thank you for the joy you bring
It always makes my heart spring

A humble person used by the Lord
Will keep all at peace and on one accord

A Praying Commitment

Help me, oh Lord, this I pray
To establish my steps in your caring way

Take away any haughtiness
That is inconsistent with your blessedness

Lead me, Lord, in the way you see best
Grant me your strength to endure any test

Fill me with wisdom for a direct impact
While keeping your precious word intact

Guide me, Lord, so I can share
With those who are lost and need your care

Anoint my words with the Holy Spirit
And give an ear to those who will hear it

A willing vessel for the battlefield
Not faint, weak, or willing to yield

Willing to serve in any way I can
Strategically following God's loving plan

Transform my life to exemplify
The example you left in your son Jesus Christ

About the Author

Crystal Y. Bullard is an author who has a heart for God, family, friends, and all walks of life. Born a California native, she was raised in Redlands where she began her love for writing poetry.

Different trials, like losing her only child after birth, challenged her to share her gift with others. Many times, during family gatherings and holidays, she shared her thoughts of love.

Crystal attended Biola University receiving a Bachelor's of Science in Organizational Leadership and the University of Phoenix receiving a Master of Science in Marriage, Family and Child Therapy.

She now resides in Nevada enjoying and dividing her time between working, writing, and encouraging others. She hopes you will get as much joy and inspiration from the poetry as she has writing it for all of you.